THE HIDDEN SECRETS OF IMMORTALITY - KATHA UPANISHAD RETOLD

The Hidden Secrets of Immortality - Katha Upanishad Retold

DR SURABHI SOLANKI

First Printing, 2025

Contents

Preface

From the Author

When I first read the *Katha Upanishad*, I did not see it as an ancient text — I heard it as a whisper.
A whisper that rose from the depths of human consciousness, speaking across millennia to anyone who has ever asked:
"Is there something within me that cannot die?"

As a doctor, I have seen life at its most fragile — the moments when breath becomes precious and time becomes visible. As a seeker, I have watched how that same breath carries something eternal — awareness, love, a mysterious presence that refuses to vanish even in the face of death.

This book was born from that intersection: **where mortality meets the immortal.**

Why Retell the Katha Upanishad Now

In today's restless world, we speak endlessly about longevity, success, and performance — yet remain silent about the one reality that shadows them all: *death.*
The ancients were not afraid to look directly at it. They saw in death not an enemy, but a teacher — the ultimate revealer of truth.

The *Katha Upanishad* is not a scripture of despair; it is a hymn to awakening.
It reminds us that immortality is not about escaping life or pro-

longing it indefinitely, but about discovering what never began and therefore can never end.

I wanted to retell this wisdom not as translation, but as **transmission** —
to render it in the living language of the 21st century, where science, spirituality, and soul can once again converse.

A Guide for the Modern Seeker

This is not a book to be "understood"; it is a book to be *entered.*
Each chapter is a doorway.
Each reflection a quiet invitation to turn inward, to listen between your own thoughts, and to remember that awareness itself — *your awareness* — is eternal.

My intention is not to teach, but to remind.
You already know what this book speaks of.
You have known it since childhood, in moments of wonder, in dreams of infinity, in silences you could never explain.

This is your remembrance.

A Note on Voice

I have written in my own voice — not as a scholar, but as a companion on the same path.
I bow to the sages who preserved these teachings,
to Yama, the fierce guardian of truth,
and to Nachiketa, the eternal seeker within every human heart.

If this book brings you closer to that quiet fire within — the flame that neither wind nor time can extinguish — then it has fulfilled its purpose.

Let us walk together, you and I, through these pages —
not toward some distant paradise,
but toward the center of the soul,
where the immortal resides,
waiting to be remembered.

— Surabhi

Prologue

There are moments in life when the world falls silent — not the silence of peace, but the silence of realization. A pause between breaths, between heartbeats, where time itself seems to dissolve. In that pause, we encounter the question that has followed humanity since the dawn of awareness:

"What lies beyond death?"

It is not merely a question of survival, but of meaning. We sense, beneath all our striving, a presence — something indestructible, untouched by decay, something that watches our life unfold and yet remains unseen. The ancients called it *Ātman*, the Self. The Katha Upanishad called it the secret of immortality.

The story begins with a boy — **Nachiketa**, young yet fearless, pure in his inquiry. He dares to ask the Lord of Death the one question every sage, scientist, and seeker has tried to answer in their own way:

"What happens after we die? Is there anything that remains?"

This is not the story of a boy and a god. It is the story of *you and me* — the seeker and the mystery, the finite and the infinite. It is the dialogue between your restless mind and your silent soul.

In every age, this question resurfaces. We disguise it behind psychology, neuroscience, or spirituality, but it is always the same longing — the desire to know what endures when everything else fades.

The Katha Upanishad does not offer belief. It offers *realization*. It does not ask us to follow a religion, but to follow our awareness inward — to the very edge of life and beyond. Its wisdom whispers that **death is not the opposite of life, but the gatekeeper of truth.**

When we begin to listen — truly listen — to this whisper of the eternal, life transforms.

We begin to see that immortality is not about living forever in time; it is about awakening to that which is *timeless* within us.

We no longer seek to escape death — we begin to *understand* it, to see it as a teacher.

And through understanding death, we discover what it truly means to live.

This book is a journey — not into doctrine, but into *direct knowing.*

Each chapter unfolds a layer of the hidden conversation between Nachiketa and Yama — between your soul and the universe — reframed for our modern world, yet faithful to the ancient current that still runs beneath it.

It is my offering to you — the reader who feels there must be more to existence than the noise of becoming.

Come. Let us walk together through the valley of questions, into the light that never dies.

The Whisper of the Eternal

The Yearning That Begins Every Journey

There is a hunger in the human heart that no possession, success, or relationship can satisfy.

It is not the hunger of the body, nor the longing of the mind — it is the call of the *soul* seeking to remember its own vastness. This yearning is the beginning of the spiritual journey, and it whispers to us from the moment we realize that everything we love will one day pass.

We may not name it, but we feel it — in the stillness after loss, in the quiet ache after achieving everything we thought we wanted.

That ache is not emptiness. It is the soul's way of reminding us that the finite can never fulfill the infinite within us.

The Restlessness of Being

The sages of old called this restlessness *Viveka* — the dawning of discernment. It is the subtle awareness that there is something *more*.

When this awareness arises, life can never be the same again. You may still move through the motions of your daily life, but a silent observer awakens inside you — questioning, watching, seeking.

This restlessness is not a curse; it is grace in disguise.

For most people, the journey toward immortality does not begin with meditation or philosophy — it begins with *discomfort*.

A sense that something essential is missing, though nothing seems wrong.

That discomfort is the divine calling you home.

The Ancient Mirror

The Katha Upanishad begins with a father and son — a moment of anger, a misunderstanding, and a destiny that would shape eternal philosophy.

The boy, Nachiketa, sees through the hollowness of ritual — the offering of old, useless cows as sacrifice.

He questions his father's act and, in doing so, questions the very foundation of human pretense.

When he asks, "To whom will you give me, Father?" he is not being rebellious — he is awakening.

For he knows, even as a child, that truth demands sincerity.

He stands as a mirror to all of us who perform the rituals of life — careers, social roles, ambitions — without asking what they truly mean.

Every seeker must one day become Nachiketa: fearless enough to ask uncomfortable questions.

The Turning Point of Inquiry

Spiritual life begins the moment we stop running from our questions.

In the modern world, we are trained to silence inquiry — to distract ourselves with entertainment, productivity, or constant movement.

But the Katha Upanishad begins with a radical act of stillness.

Nachiketa waits three nights at the doorstep of Death.

He waits without food, without comfort, without distraction — a metaphor for the inner state of the seeker.

When the mind no longer runs after pleasure or fear, the deeper truth begins to reveal itself.

To wait in silence before the unknown — that is the first step toward immortality.

The Death of the Superficial

Every authentic transformation demands a kind of death — not of the body, but of illusion.

We must allow the shallow layers of identity to fade: our titles, beliefs, and fears of loss.

Only when the false dies can the real begin to shine through.

This is the meaning of *Yama* — not the grim reaper, but the cosmic intelligence that dissolves everything impermanent.

Death, in this sacred context, is not a punishment but purification.

It removes what cannot endure, revealing what always has.

Your Own Nachiketa Moment

Every reader, at some point in life, encounters their Nachiketa moment — when comfort no longer comforts, and life demands authenticity.

It may come through heartbreak, illness, failure, or simply an existential fatigue that whispers, "Is this all there is?"

When that moment comes, remember: it is not despair. It is initiation.

The soul uses dissatisfaction to awaken you.

You are being called, as Nachiketa was, to stand before your own "Yama" — to face the fear that hides the truth.

Immortality does not begin in temples or scriptures.

It begins in that moment when you stop pretending and begin to ask, *"Who am I really?"*

Reflection Practice

Tonight, sit in silence and listen for the whisper beneath your thoughts.

Ask yourself — not with the mind, but with the heart:

"What in me does not change?"

Do not seek an answer.

The question itself is the beginning of remembrance.

Nachiketa's Courage

The Seeker Who Dared to Question Death

Every true seeker begins with courage — not the courage to fight the world, but the courage to face oneself.

Nachiketa's story is not about a boy confronting Death; it is about a soul confronting illusion.

It is the moment when consciousness refuses to remain asleep, when it chooses truth over comfort, and awakening over approval.

The Birth of Courage

Nachiketa's courage did not arise from defiance; it arose from clarity.

He saw, even as a young boy, that the rituals of his father's sacrifice were hollow — that giving away old, dying cows could never fulfill the sacred purpose of offering.

He questioned not to rebel, but to understand.

His father, bound by social pride, reacted in anger: *"To Death I give you!"*

Yet the words that escaped in fury became prophecy.

Thus begins the soul's journey — born not of harmony, but of friction between truth and appearance.

In that moment, Nachiketa stepped across the threshold of ordinary life.

He became the *seeker*, and his father — representing the old consciousness — symbolized the world that clings to form while forgetting essence.

The Courage to Ask

We often imagine courage as bold action — yet the greatest courage is *honest questioning.*

To question your beliefs, your identity, your own conditioned patterns — this is far more terrifying than confronting any external threat.

Because the moment you question deeply, the ego trembles.

It knows that inquiry is the beginning of its end.

Nachiketa's question, "To whom will you give me?" is not a child's complaint.

It is a cosmic question, echoing through every age:

"Who owns me? Who do I belong to? What is the reality to which I must surrender?"

Every seeker must ask this — for the soul's freedom begins when it realizes it has been living in the house of borrowed truths.

Facing Death — The Ultimate Teacher

When Nachiketa arrives at Yama's abode, he finds the Lord of Death absent.

So he waits — three nights without food, without comfort, without distraction.

This is symbolic of the three layers of human consciousness he must pass through before wisdom reveals itself:

1. **The Physical** – endurance beyond the body's cravings.
2. **The Emotional** – peace beyond the heart's longing.

3. **The Mental** – stillness beyond thought's turbulence.

Only when these three fires are endured does the divine response awaken.
Yama appears not as punishment, but as revelation — for when the seeker becomes ready, the teacher must appear.

Death as the Mirror of Life

In modern times, we fear death because we do not understand it.
We have made death an enemy, forgetting that it is only the shadow of life.
The Upanishad invites us to look deeper: if death can exist, then what *dies*? And what *remains*?

Nachiketa did not run away.
He did not beg for life, for wealth, or for escape.
He simply waited — eyes open, heart awake, accepting the unknown.

That is the true mark of spiritual maturity:
To sit before the void without panic.
To allow truth to approach in its own rhythm.
To trust that existence, in its mystery, is ultimately benevolent.

The Three Boons

When Yama finally appears, he offers Nachiketa three boons — a profound metaphor for the stages of spiritual evolution.

1. **The First Boon – Reconciliation with the Father:**
   The healing of the personal. Before seeking truth, one must make peace with the past.
   Forgiveness clears the inner path.
2. **The Second Boon – The Fire of Sacrifice:**
   The understanding of the sacred discipline — how ac-

tion, intention, and devotion become offerings that prepare consciousness for higher realization.

3. **The Third Boon – The Question of Death:**
   The final inquiry: *"What happens after death? Does the soul still exist?"*
   Here the seeker transcends the personal and enters the universal.

In these three boons lies the map of every seeker's path — healing the personal, refining the spiritual practice, and finally, dissolving into the infinite.

Modern Parallels – Courage in Our Time

Today, Nachiketa's courage takes new forms.
It is the courage of a scientist who questions assumptions,
the artist who confronts truth through beauty,
the individual who resists conformity to follow their inner knowing.

In every field, courage is the same flame — the willingness to see without distortion.
Each time you ask a question that threatens your comfort, you are living the spirit of Nachiketa.

The Inner Yama

Yama is not outside. He is the aspect of consciousness that tests your readiness.
When you decide to grow, life will challenge your attachments, your illusions, and your fears.
These are your "three nights."
If you can endure them with patience and awareness, wisdom will reveal itself naturally.

The dialogue between Nachiketa and Yama is the eternal conversation between the evolving soul and the divine intelligence that governs transformation.

The seeker and Death are not enemies; they are partners in awakening.

Reflection Practice

Tonight, reflect on the questions that life has been asking *you*.

What patterns are ending?
What illusions are dying?
What truths are demanding your attention?

Sit with these without resistance.
Let Yama speak — not as fear, but as freedom.

Courage is not the absence of fear.
It is the refusal to let fear dictate the boundaries of truth.

The Threshold of the Fire

The Purification of the Seeker

When Nachiketa asks Yama for his second boon — to learn the sacred fire that leads to heaven — he is not seeking a ritual, but *a revelation.*

The "fire" (*Agni*) of the Katha Upanishad is not the flame that consumes wood; it is the fire that consumes ignorance.

It is the divine alchemy through which desire becomes devotion, action becomes offering, and the mortal self awakens to immortality.

Fire, in all spiritual traditions, symbolizes transformation.

It is the one element that can never be polluted — whatever enters it is purified.

So too must the seeker's consciousness pass through the fire of awareness, until all that is false is turned to ash and only the radiant Self remains.

The Three Fires Within

The Upanishads speak of the fire as both **outer** and **inner**.

In the sacred ritual, Agni bridges earth and heaven.

In the inner life, it connects the human and the divine.

There are **three fires** within every seeker:

1. **The Fire of Aspiration (*Icchā Agni*)** – the yearning to know truth. This is the first spark that awakens the soul.
2. **The Fire of Discipline (*Tapas Agni*)** – the heat of purification, where distractions and attachments are burned away.
3. **The Fire of Knowledge (*Jñāna Agni*)** – the luminous understanding that reveals the eternal Self.

Nachiketa's request to learn the sacred fire is symbolic of mastering all three — of learning how to *tend* the flame rather than be consumed by it.

The Symbolism of the Sacred Fire

Yama teaches Nachiketa the exact form of the fire — the altar, the arrangement, the sacred chant.

But this is only the outer teaching.

The true "altar" is built within the heart.

The offering is one's ego, the fuel is awareness, and the flame is the light of consciousness.

When the seeker learns to live in constant remembrance — every act, every thought offered into the fire of awareness — life itself becomes a yajña, a sacred sacrifice.

This is the meaning of the fire that leads to heaven:

When life is lived as offering, every action becomes liberation.

The Law of Transformation

Fire does not destroy; it transforms.

It takes form and returns it to essence.

Likewise, spiritual practice does not remove life's experiences — it transforms how we relate to them.

Pain becomes purification.

Loss becomes learning.

Desire becomes direction.

This is the secret Yama gives: there is no need to run from the world.
The same fire that burns can also illumine — if one learns how to offer.

Modern Fire – The Inner Alchemy

In our times, the sacred fire takes subtler forms.
It is the *burning question* that will not leave you.
It is the creative urge that transforms suffering into art.
It is the silent discipline of awareness that keeps your heart awake amid chaos.

When you sit in meditation and face the restlessness of your mind without escape, you are feeding the sacred fire.
When you act selflessly in a world obsessed with reward, you are building the altar of Agni.
And when you see beauty even in endings, you are touching immortality.

The Fire as Teacher

In the Upanishad, Yama names this fire after Nachiketa — *Nachiketa Agni* — because the fire becomes one with the seeker who understands it.
Every true student eventually becomes the teaching itself.
The knowledge no longer remains borrowed; it burns from within.

The teacher, too, is only a spark-giver — one who lights your inner fire and then steps aside.
This is why Yama, the Lord of Death, becomes the Lord of Enlightenment — he destroys only what must die for the light to be born.

The Sacred Equation

The wisdom of the fire can be expressed as a simple equation:

Awareness + Offering = Transformation

Whatever you are aware of and offer without resistance transforms into freedom.
Whatever you cling to in ignorance binds you further.

This is the essence of karma yoga, of tapas, of devotion — all unified in the symbol of fire.
The fire of consciousness consumes separation.

Crossing the Threshold

Nachiketa, having learned the sacred fire, stands purified — ready for the third and final boon.
He has reconciled with the personal (first boon), mastered the sacred (second boon), and now stands at the edge of the eternal (third boon).
He is the purified vessel through which the truth of immortality will soon be revealed.

The Upanishad uses fire as the threshold because no one crosses into the infinite without passing through purification.
The impurities are not sins — they are simply shadows of forgetfulness.
When they are burned, the soul remembers its own light.

Reflection Practice

Light a candle or a small lamp.
Gaze at its flame for a few minutes.
As you do, whisper inwardly:

"May this fire burn all that is false in me.
May it reveal the Self that never dies."

Then close your eyes.
Feel that same flame glowing in your heart — steady, bright, silent.
That is *your* Nachiketa Agni — the fire that leads beyond death.

Meeting Yama

The Lord of Limits and the Guardian of Wisdom

There is a moment in every seeker's life when truth steps out of abstraction and takes form.

For Nachiketa, that moment came when Yama — the Lord of Death — appeared before him.

Yet the meeting was not a confrontation with terror; it was a meeting with *clarity itself.*

Yama is not the destroyer we imagine.

He is the **custodian of cosmic order**, the guardian of the threshold that separates ignorance from realization.

To meet Yama is to meet the law — the silent principle that governs both life and death, holding the balance of all existence.

The True Nature of Yama

In Sanskrit, *Yama* comes from the root *yam*, meaning "to control, to restrain, to regulate."

He is the divine intelligence that imposes limits so that consciousness may evolve through form.

Without Yama, there would be chaos — infinite energy with no direction.

Through Yama, the infinite learns to dance within boundaries.

Yama's realm is not the graveyard, but the **universe of laws** — the laws of karma, rhythm, birth, and decay.

He does not punish; he educates.

He does not end life; he reveals that which cannot end.

When we truly understand Yama, fear dissolves — for we see that death is only the universe's way of keeping time in eternity.

The First Test of the Seeker

When Yama returns and sees Nachiketa waiting patiently after three nights of silence, he is moved.

Patience itself is the first initiation.

The restless mind that once sought answers has now learned stillness — and only in stillness can truth descend.

Yama offers three boons, and after granting the first two, he listens as Nachiketa asks the question that has haunted every heart since the beginning of time:

"When a person dies, some say they exist; others say they do not.

Tell me, what truly happens after death?"

This is the question that cracks open the universe.

Yama's Refusal

Yama smiles.

He recognizes the depth of Nachiketa's inquiry — but also the danger.

The knowledge of immortality cannot be given to the unready; it must be *earned through understanding.*

So Yama tests him.

He offers every imaginable pleasure: long life, wealth, music, companionship, kingdoms, celestial delights.

All the gifts of the transient world are laid before the boy.

"Choose these," Yama says, "and live well. Do not ask about death."

But Nachiketa sees through the illusion.

He answers with words that echo through eternity:

"All these pleasures wear out the senses, O Death.

Even the longest life is short.

Keep thy chariots, keep thy dance and song.
I choose only that which is eternal."

The Courage to Refuse the World

Here lies the essence of renunciation — not withdrawal from life, but freedom from its hypnotic glamour.

Nachiketa's refusal is not ascetic; it is awakened discernment (*viveka*).

He sees that pleasure is time-bound, and anything time-bound cannot satisfy the timeless soul.

This is the seeker's second great courage: the ability to say *no* — not out of suppression, but out of wisdom.

For to refuse the transient is to invite the eternal.

In that one moment, Nachiketa becomes worthy of the highest knowledge.

His clarity becomes the mirror through which Yama must now reveal the truth.

Yama as the Inner Teacher

Yama is not an external god to be feared; he is the **voice of discrimination within**.

He appears whenever we are ready to transcend illusion.

He is the force that strips away comfort, forcing us to look beyond surface reality.

In our own lives, Yama arrives as the moment of loss, the breakup, the illness, the failure — every experience that removes false identity.

When we stop fighting these moments and begin to listen, we realize:

The destroyer was the teacher all along.

Yama teaches through negation.

By showing us what perishes, he reveals what does not.

He is the mirror of impermanence in which the immortal is finally seen.

The Law of Limits

In the Upanishadic vision, the divine expresses itself through polarity: birth and death, light and darkness, growth and decay. Yama embodies the principle of **limit** — the boundary that makes experience possible.

Without death, life would lose meaning; without endings, there could be no evolution.

When we embrace limit as sacred, we discover freedom within form.

The goal of spiritual life is not to escape the law but to align with it — to flow so harmoniously with existence that even boundaries become expressions of infinity.

This is what the ancients called *dharma* — the cosmic order in motion.

The Modern Yama

In our age, Yama manifests not as myth but as *awareness of impermanence.*

Every time technology accelerates life, every time we chase novelty, Yama whispers:

"Remember, this too shall pass."

To live wisely is not to escape this truth, but to harmonize with it.

Modern spirituality often seeks eternity in the continuation of the body or the mind, but true immortality lies in realizing that which observes both.

Death teaches us presence.

When we see that everything changes, we stop postponing life.

The awareness of limit awakens the intensity of *now.*

The Blessing of the Lord of Death

When Yama finally grants the third boon, he reveals not information but insight.

He does not describe heaven or the afterlife; he unveils the Self that transcends both.

For immortality is not the continuation of experience — it is the recognition of that which is beyond all experience.

Thus, the Lord of Death becomes the **Lord of Immortality** — the one who destroys ignorance by unveiling the eternal.

Reflection Practice

Sit in a quiet place and contemplate:

"What in my life is changing?
What in me observes that change?"

See if you can sense the still witness behind the passing flow of time.

That witness — silent, untouched, eternal — is your own *Yama consciousness*.

It is not against you; it is guiding you home.

Closing Insight

To meet Yama is to meet the truth of existence —
that life and death are two breaths of the same Being.

Fear arises only when we identify with the breath;
freedom begins when we recognize the air itself.

The Temptations of the Finite

Choosing Between the Good and the Pleasant

Every seeker who approaches truth must face a test — not from an external authority, but from life itself.

This test is ancient, universal, and subtle. It is the choice between two paths:

Preyas — the pleasant

Shreyas — the good

Yama calls this the first and final decision of every soul.

One leads to temporary delight and deeper bondage; the other leads to discipline, purification, and liberation.

The Eternal Choice

Yama says to Nachiketa:

"The good and the pleasant approach man. The wise choose the good; the foolish, through love of pleasure, choose the pleasant."

This is not a moral instruction — it is a description of consciousness.

Each moment, we are given both: the glitter of immediacy and the glow of truth.

The pleasant seduces; the good transforms.

Preyas promises satisfaction *now*, while Shreyas offers fulfillment *forever.*

But the path of the good demands patience, clarity, and courage — the qualities of Nachiketa's heart.

The Nature of Preyas

Preyas is the pull of the senses, the momentum of habit, the hunger for validation and comfort.

It whispers:

"Enjoy now; understand later."

It feeds on distraction, promising quick relief from the anxiety of existence.

But Preyas never ends; it renews its hunger endlessly.

Like a mirage, it keeps the traveler walking but never quenches thirst.

In the modern world, Preyas takes infinite forms — the constant scroll of attention, the addiction to novelty, the performance of identity.

It tells us that happiness is something to be achieved, rather than realized.

But every indulgence that forgets the eternal increases the soul's forgetfulness.

The Nature of Shreyas

Shreyas, the path of the good, speaks softly.

It does not glitter — it *glows.*

It invites reflection instead of reaction.

It says:

"What leads you closer to truth may not feel pleasant, but it will bring peace."

Choosing Shreyas is not repression; it is liberation from compulsion.

It means acting from awareness rather than impulse.

It requires a deeper intelligence — the ability to see beyond the surface of events.

When we align with Shreyas, our lives become an offering rather than an appetite.

Action becomes sacred; stillness becomes strength.

The Inner Battlefield

The battle between Preyas and Shreyas happens not outside, but within the mind.

Every thought, every decision, is a crossroad.

One road moves toward remembrance of the Self; the other toward further entanglement in the world of appearances.

When the mind is restless, Preyas appears irresistible.

When the mind is still, Shreyas reveals its quiet majesty.

Thus, the spiritual path is not a war against pleasure, but a refinement of perception — learning to distinguish the fleeting from the lasting.

Nachiketa's Clarity

When Yama tempts Nachiketa with wealth, beauty, and longevity, the boy sees through the illusion instantly.

His vision is not one of suppression but of wisdom.

He knows that no amount of sensory pleasure can answer the question, *"Who am I?"*

His words to Yama are the essence of all spiritual renunciation:

"Even the longest life is short. Keep thy pleasures, O Death. Tell me only that which endures beyond decay."

In that one sentence, the Upanishad distills the difference between religion and realization.

Religion bargains for heaven; realization demands truth.

Modern Reflections – The Digital Temptation

Today's world amplifies Preyas to its maximum volume.

Every screen, every advertisement, every algorithm whispers: *"This will complete you."*

But the Upanishadic wisdom reminds us — no object can fulfill a subject.

The joy we seek in things is only a reflection of the bliss we have forgotten within ourselves.

Choosing Shreyas in our time may look like simplicity, mindfulness, authenticity, or courage to be silent in a noisy world.
It means valuing stillness over stimulation, depth over distraction, essence over appearance.

Every act of conscious living — from choosing truth in conversation to choosing purpose over popularity — is a Nachiketa moment.

The Science of Subtle Choice

On a deeper level, Preyas and Shreyas represent two energies within the psyche:

- **Preyas** arises from the lower mind (*manas*) — reactive, sensory, and outward-seeking.
- **Shreyas** arises from the higher intellect (*buddhi*) — discriminative, inward, and reflective.

The secret of mastery is to make the *buddhi* the charioteer of your life.
When intellect guides and senses obey, the journey becomes smooth.
When senses rule and intellect sleeps, chaos reigns.

Thus, Yama is training Nachiketa — and through him, all of us — in the **art of alignment.**

Freedom Through Awareness

The choice between the good and the pleasant is not a moral judgment but an awakening of awareness.
When you see clearly, choice becomes effortless.
You do not *resist* the pleasant; you simply *outgrow* it.

It is like a child giving up toys not out of guilt, but because they no longer satisfy.
In the same way, when awareness deepens, shallow pleasures

lose their grip.

Joy arises from within, and the world becomes a mirror of that joy.

The Wisdom of Yama

Yama teaches not by forbidding but by revealing.

He shows the seeker that the path of Shreyas is not renunciation of life, but a deeper embrace of it — with full consciousness.

Pleasure is no longer denied, but purified.

Action is no longer mechanical, but mindful.

Love is no longer attachment, but offering.

Thus, Yama transforms from the Lord of Death into the **Master of Liberation.**

Reflection Practice

Throughout the day, pause before each major decision — however small — and ask:

"Is this Preyas or Shreyas?"

"Will this bring momentary excitement, or enduring peace?"

Write down what you notice.

You will begin to see that most choices are invitations to awareness.

And that awareness, once kindled, becomes the fire that purifies all action.

Closing Insight

The path of Shreyas is the quiet rebellion of the soul.

It is the refusal to be hypnotized by impermanence.

Every time you choose awareness over impulse, truth over comfort, silence over noise —

you choose immortality over illusion.

That is the hidden secret Yama wished for all humanity to learn.

The Silence Between Worlds

Turning Inward to the Self

There comes a point on the seeker's path when all words grow thin, all reasoning quiets, and one realizes that truth cannot be found in thought.

Nachiketa, having passed through Yama's tests, stands now in this silence — not a silence of absence, but of fullness.

It is here, between the seen and unseen, between life and death, that the real journey begins.

The Language of Silence

The Upanishads were not written to be *read*; they were meant to be *heard* in silence.

Their wisdom flows not through sound, but through the stillness *after* sound — the gap where truth reveals itself.

This is the "mauna," the sacred silence, where the limited mind bows before the boundless Self.

Silence is not the absence of activity.

It is the presence of awareness.

It is the moment when the seeker stops asking "What is real?" and begins to *experience* reality directly.

The Inner Turn

Yama tells Nachiketa:

"The Self cannot be known by study, nor by intellect, nor by hearing from others.
It is known by him whom It chooses — to such a one, the Self reveals Its own nature."

This is the point where philosophy becomes realization.
The intellect can guide us to the door, but only silence opens it.

Meditation is not a technique; it is surrender — the art of ceasing to interfere with what *is*.
In stillness, we cease chasing thoughts, and instead turn awareness upon awareness.
This turning inward is the soul's homecoming.

Crossing the Boundary of the Mind

The mind, Yama teaches, is the bridge between mortality and immortality.
When the mind is outward-turned, it sees only fragments.
When it turns inward, it sees the source of all.

Imagine a lake.
When the surface is disturbed, the moon's reflection shatters.
When the lake becomes still, the moon shines perfectly.
Likewise, when the mind is restless, truth appears broken.
When the mind becomes still, the eternal Self is revealed.

This is the silence between worlds — the stillness between breaths, between thoughts, where the mortal dissolves into the immortal.

The Death of Noise

In our time, noise has become the new oxygen.
We fill every moment with sound, every silence with distraction.
The modern mind fears quiet because quiet reveals truth — and truth demands transformation.

But real meditation begins when one allows noise to die.
When the constant commentary of "me" falls away, what remains is *being*.

That being has no beginning or end — it is the awareness that witnessed your birth and will remain untouched by your death.

When you rest in that awareness, you cross from time into eternity.

The Two Selves

Yama explains to Nachiketa that within every being reside two selves:

1. **The Lower Self (*Jīvātman*)** — the personality, bound by desire and memory, that identifies with body and thought.
2. **The Higher Self (*Paramātman*)** — the witnessing consciousness that never changes, never dies, and never acts.

The purpose of life is not to destroy the lower, but to *recognize* the higher within it.

When the limited self bows to the infinite, the two become one — and death loses its meaning.

This is the great revelation hidden in silence:

The one who dies is never who you truly are.

The Practice of Deep Listening

To enter the silence between worlds, one must learn the art of *listening* — not with the ears, but with the heart.

Listening without interpretation, without grasping, without the need to respond.

In that deep listening, the inner noise of thought softens, and the sacred hum of existence becomes audible.

In yogic tradition, this is called *nāda* — the inner sound of consciousness, the vibration of being itself.

To hear it is to realize that the entire universe is made of awareness vibrating as life.

Silence, then, is not the absence of sound — it is the origin of all sound.

Modern Meditation – The Still Revolution

Meditation has become a global word, often stripped of its sacred meaning.

It is not relaxation, nor escapism.

It is a rebellion — a gentle revolution against unconscious living.

To meditate is to refuse the hypnosis of constant doing.

It is to remember that behind every thought, every emotion, there is a witness untouched.

When you sit in silence, you are meeting that witness — the one Yama revealed to Nachiketa, the immortal Self that watches worlds rise and fall without being changed.

The Doorway Between Life and Death

The Upanishads speak of a moment at the threshold of death — the final inhalation, when breath pauses before releasing into infinity.

That pause is the same stillness we touch in meditation.

The wise learn to die before they die — by entering that stillness daily.

For one who knows the Self in life, death becomes merely another breath of eternity.

This is why the sages said:

"He who knows the Self while living, for him death does not exist."

To meditate, then, is to rehearse immortality.

Reflection Practice

Sit comfortably.

Close your eyes and bring your attention to your breath.

Notice the pause between inhalation and exhalation.

Rest in that pause — not clinging to the breath, not resisting it.

In that gap, awareness shines — silent, formless, infinite.

That stillness is your true nature.

You are not in the silence.

You are the silence.

Closing Insight

Between one breath and the next lies eternity.

Between one thought and the next lies the Self.

To dwell there — even for a moment — is to touch the deathless.

It is the silence between worlds, where the soul remembers its original song.

The Hidden Flame

Knowing the Self

In every being there burns a flame — subtle, silent, and unseen.

It neither flickers with the wind of change nor fades with the passage of time.

This flame is not of matter, but of awareness.

It is the *Ātman*, the Self — the eternal witness that illumines all experience yet remains untouched by any of it.

Yama calls this the greatest secret, the "hidden flame within the heart."

Nachiketa, purified by inquiry and silence, is now ready to receive its revelation.

The Flame in the Heart

The Upanishad declares:

"The Self is smaller than the smallest, greater than the greatest, hidden in the hearts of all creatures."

In this paradox lies the essence of truth.

The Self is beyond measurement because it is the *source* of measurement.

It is subtler than the atom, vaster than the cosmos.

It pervades every cell, yet transcends every form.

When you close your eyes and sense a still presence behind all thoughts, that is the flame the sages spoke of — the *pratyagātman*, the inward light.

The Mirror of Awareness

Imagine a beam of light shining through a prism.
It appears as many colors, yet all colors are but expressions of the same white radiance.
Similarly, consciousness refracted through the prism of mind appears as "I," "you," "this," and "that."
But behind all diversity burns the same Self — one flame, many reflections.

The mind is the mirror in which awareness sees itself.
When the mirror is clear, you recognize your divinity.
When it is clouded by desire and fear, you mistake reflection for reality.

Yama's teaching to Nachiketa is not that the soul *has* light — but that the soul *is* light.

The Nature of the Self

The Self cannot be grasped by the intellect, for the intellect itself shines by Its light.
Yama explains:

"The sun does not shine there, nor the moon, nor the stars, nor lightning —
all these borrow their light from the Self."

It is because of the Self that the eyes can see,
the mind can think,
and life can move.

The Self is not an object to be known;
it is the *knower* of all objects.
It cannot be seen, because it is the *seeing itself.*

The Modern Paradox – Searching for What You Already Are

In our age, humanity searches for selfhood in countless ways — through identity, success, creativity, and relationships.
But all these are *expressions* of the Self, not the Self itself.

The more we search outward, the more we move away from what we seek.
The Self cannot be found because it has never been lost — only obscured by noise.

To "know the Self" is not to add knowledge; it is to drop misidentification.
It is not an acquisition but a recognition — the remembrance of what has always been true.

The Flame and the Shadow

Yama teaches that ignorance (*avidyā*) is the shadow cast by the flame of awareness when it identifies with form.
When consciousness forgets itself, it becomes entangled in time and fear.
But when it remembers, even for a moment, the illusion of death dissolves.

For the Self was never born, and therefore can never die.

Birth and death belong to the body,
change belongs to the mind,
but the witness remains untouched — like the sky through which clouds pass.

The Science of Immortality

In the Upanishadic view, immortality is not endless existence in time — it is *existence beyond time.*
The Self does not continue; it *is.*
It was before birth, it remains after death, and it shines through every moment in between.

Modern science hints at this truth when it tells us that energy cannot be created or destroyed — only transformed.
But the sages went further: awareness itself, the knower of energy, is beyond all transformation.

It is the unchanging background against which the entire universe flickers and fades.

The Flame in Daily Life

To live in awareness of the Self is not to withdraw from life, but to infuse every act with consciousness.

When you walk, know that the walker, the walking, and the path are all illumined by the same flame.

When you speak, remember that the speaker and the listener are one awareness in dialogue with itself.

When you love, know that love is the recognition of unity shining through two forms.

This is how the ancient truth becomes a living experience — not in temples or rituals, but in the way you inhabit every breath.

The Teacher's Blessing

Having revealed the Self, Yama concludes:

"This Self is not attained by instruction, nor by intellect, nor by much hearing.

It is attained only by him whom It chooses.

To him, the Self reveals Its own nature."

What does it mean that the Self "chooses"?

It means that realization is not forced; it unfolds naturally when the seeker becomes empty enough to receive.

When the ego's noise subsides, the Self shines by its own grace —

not as a reward, but as revelation.

The Flame of Compassion

Knowing the Self transforms not only perception, but relationship.

When you recognize that the same consciousness lives in all beings, compassion arises effortlessly.

You no longer love out of need, but out of recognition.

You no longer harm, for to harm another is to harm yourself.

The awakened life is not withdrawal — it is participation in unity.
It is fire without smoke — light without attachment.

Reflection Practice

Close your eyes and bring your attention to the center of your chest.
Visualize a flame there — steady, radiant, gentle.
With each breath, feel its warmth expand through your entire being.

Repeat inwardly:

"I am the light that illumines all."

Do not imagine it; *remember* it.
For this is not a visualization — it is recognition of what already is.

Closing Insight

The Self is not somewhere to reach; it is what remains when all reaching ends.
It is the hidden flame that makes you alive, aware, and free.
When you see that this flame burns in all — in stone, in star, in stranger, in self —
you will understand what immortality truly means.

It is not the endless continuation of the body.
It is the unbroken continuity of consciousness —
the fire that neither begins nor ends,
but only shines.

The Chariot of the Soul

Mastering the Mind and the Senses

Among all the metaphors in the Upanishads, few are as vivid and profound as the one Yama now reveals to Nachiketa — the **chariot of the soul**.

In it lies the secret of inner mastery, self-realization, and ultimately, freedom from death.

Yama speaks not as a poet but as a cosmic psychologist, describing the precise structure of human consciousness — its vehicles, drivers, and passengers.

This allegory is not only ancient; it is timeless, offering us a complete map of spiritual evolution, as relevant now as it was thousands of years ago.

The Architecture of the Chariot

Yama tells Nachiketa:

"Know the Self as the master of the chariot,
the body as the chariot itself,
the intellect as the charioteer,
and the mind as the reins.

The senses are the horses,
the objects of the senses are the roads.

When the Self is joined with the body, mind, and senses,
the wise call him the enjoyer."

This allegory reveals the multi-layered reality of human existence — from the eternal driver to the restless steeds.
Let us understand each part deeply.

The Self — The Master of the Chariot

At the heart of it all sits the **Self**, the silent witness — untouched by movement yet the source of all direction.
It does not act, yet all actions occur in Its presence.
It neither comes nor goes, but through It, all journeys unfold.

The Self is pure awareness — the eternal traveler who takes up countless vehicles (bodies, lifetimes, experiences) to rediscover its own perfection.
This is *Ātman*, the soul's immortal essence.

The Body — The Chariot

The body is the sacred vehicle through which consciousness experiences the world.
It is not to be despised, but respected — maintained, guided, and used with awareness.
A chariot well-built can take the traveler far; one neglected will break on the road.

The Upanishadic seers did not reject the body; they sanctified it as the temple of the Self.
The wise care for it not as vanity, but as stewardship.

The Intellect — The Charioteer

The **intellect (*buddhi*)** is the driver — the capacity for discrimination, reasoning, and direction.
It knows the map of dharma, the laws of right movement.
If the charioteer is skilled, the journey is smooth; if he is careless or asleep, chaos follows.

In the modern world, many live with intellects untutored by wisdom — brilliant minds without inner direction.
Yama warns that intellect must serve awareness, not ego.

Otherwise, intelligence becomes cleverness — steering the soul into endless circles.

The Mind — The Reins

The **mind (*manas*)** connects intellect to senses — it is the reins that communicate command.

When the reins are firm and steady, the horses obey.

When they are loose or frayed, the chariot veers off course.

The mind's restlessness, its constant chatter, is the primary cause of spiritual drift.

Meditation is the art of holding the reins gently yet firmly — guiding thought without suppression, allowing awareness to lead rather than react.

The Senses — The Horses

The **senses** are the five horses pulling the chariot — sight, sound, taste, touch, and smell.

They are powerful, eager, and wild.

If left untrained, they chase every object they see, dragging the chariot through endless detours of desire.

But when disciplined and directed, the senses become allies of awakening.

A well-trained horse does not lose its strength; it learns precision.

So too, the spiritual seeker learns not to deny the senses, but to master them — to let them serve rather than enslave.

The Roads — The Sense Objects

The world of experience — sounds, sights, pleasures, ideas — forms the roads upon which the chariot travels.

The journey itself is not the problem; it is *identification* that creates bondage.

When you forget that you are the traveler and become lost in the scenery, you lose your way.

The world is not to be escaped, but navigated — consciously, gracefully, awake.

The Two Journeys

Yama distinguishes between two travelers:

1. **The Untrained Traveler**

"He whose mind is unrestrained,
whose intellect is not illumined —
his senses are ungoverned,
and his soul goes astray like an uncontrolled chariot."

This traveler is the ordinary person, pulled by desires, tossed by impulses, and unaware of the Self within.

1. **The Awakened Traveler**

"He whose mind is controlled,
whose intellect is steady —
his senses are obedient,
and he reaches the end of the journey,
the abode of the Supreme."

This is the sage — the one who knows that mastery of the chariot leads to liberation from all roads.

The Inner Engineering of Freedom

In this allegory, Yama offers humanity one of the earliest models of **psychospiritual integration.**
The body, mind, and intellect are not enemies to the soul — they are instruments.
When harmonized, they create *yoga* — union between the finite and infinite.

Modern life has inverted this order: the senses lead, the mind follows, the intellect rationalizes, and the Self is forgotten.
The result is exhaustion, confusion, and alienation.
But when the order is restored — Self leading, intellect guiding, mind obeying, senses serving — peace returns.

This is the essence of self-mastery.

Training the Chariot

How can we live this wisdom today?

Yama's teaching translates beautifully into modern practice:

- **For the body (the chariot):** Care for it as a temple — through right food, rest, and movement.
- **For the senses (the horses):** Choose your inputs consciously — what you watch, read, and consume shapes your direction.
- **For the mind (the reins):** Practice stillness; silence is the strength of restraint.
- **For the intellect (the charioteer):** Study wisdom; refine discrimination through reflection and dialogue.
- **For the Self (the master):** Remember. You are not the chariot, nor the horses, nor the reins — you are the witness behind the entire movement.

When the Journey Ends

Yama concludes that when the soul reaches perfect mastery, it transcends the need for travel.

The chariot dissolves; the horses rest.

There is no longer movement from here to there, for the traveler realizes — *there was never anywhere to go.*

The journey through worlds ends in the discovery of the Self, and the seeker realizes that the destination was within all along.

Reflection Practice

Sit quietly and contemplate this:

"Am I riding the chariot of my senses,
or is the chariot riding me?"

Throughout the day, notice when the horses pull you — into reactions, temptations, or anxieties.

Gently take the reins back.

Bring awareness to the present moment and let the intellect guide with compassion.

Each time you do, the chariot steadies, and the master reclaims his seat.

Closing Insight

Mastery is not control — it is *clarity.*
The goal is not to suppress the horses, but to align them.
When all parts of your being move in harmony with awareness,
you ride not through the world,
but through the infinite —
as the chariot of God.

Crossing the River of Fear

Transforming Death into Awakening

Fear is humanity's oldest companion.
It has guided survival, guarded instincts, and shaped civilizations — but it has also chained the soul.
Every form of fear, whether subtle or raw, is a shadow of one primal terror: **the fear of death**.

Yama, the Lord of Death, teaches Nachiketa not merely about dying, but about *transcending the fear of dying*.
For to conquer this fear is to awaken into immortality — the state beyond anxiety, time, and loss.

The Birth of Fear

Fear arises wherever identification begins.
When consciousness says, "I am this body," then the body's vulnerability becomes *my* vulnerability.
When it says, "I am this mind," then every thought of rejection or loss threatens existence itself.

Thus, fear is not a condition of life — it is a condition of misidentification.
The Self, which is infinite and unbound, has mistaken itself for what is temporary and limited.

In truth, fear is not defeated; it is *dissolved* by understanding who you are.

Yama's Revelation

Yama tells Nachiketa:

"The one who sees the Self as different from the body, the mind, and the senses —
for him, sorrow and fear vanish."

In this single sentence, the Katha Upanishad transforms the entire psychology of fear.

The cause of fear is *confusion of identity.*

When you remember the Self, fear becomes irrelevant — not because danger disappears, but because *you* no longer depend on what can be destroyed.

The River of Fear

Yama describes existence as a river that all beings must cross. On one shore lies birth and attachment; on the other lies freedom and realization.

The waters in between are turbulent with the waves of desire, loss, and death.

The unawakened cross in panic, clinging to the fragile raft of possessions and promises.

But the awakened stand still in the current, realizing:

"I am not the one who crosses; I am the river itself."

This shift of identity — from the passing to the permanent — is liberation.

The Psychology of Fear in the Modern World

In today's age, death hides behind polished walls — hospitals, euphemisms, distractions.

We deny it with cosmetic youth, digital immortality, and endless entertainment.

Yet beneath the surface, the collective fear deepens.

This denial breeds anxiety — the constant low hum that haunts even the most comfortable lives.

We rush, achieve, and accumulate not because we love life, but because we dread its end.

The Upanishadic approach is the opposite: **look directly at death**.
To contemplate it is not morbid; it is medicine.
It restores perspective.
It burns illusion.
It teaches urgency — not the panic of the finite, but the precision of the eternal.

The Transformation of Death

Yama explains that death is not a destroyer but a revealer.
It removes form so that essence can shine.
Every ending is a doorway disguised as darkness.
Those who see only the loss miss the light beyond it.

Nachiketa, standing before Yama, realizes that death is not an enemy to defeat, but a mystery to embrace.
In that acceptance, fear dissolves.
He sees that birth and death are merely rhythms of the same eternal Self — inhalation and exhalation of the Infinite.

The Moment of Realization

Yama leads Nachiketa to the final truth:

"The one who knows the Self, born of the old and unborn, eternal and changeless —
he crosses beyond sorrow."

Here, *crossing* no longer means movement; it means awakening.
When the mind ceases to divide life and death, self and other, joy and pain, it discovers a stillness beyond duality.
That stillness is immortality itself.

This realization does not end physical death — it ends psychological dying, the constant contraction of fear that separates the soul from the present moment.

Fear as Fire, Awareness as Water

Fear, when faced, becomes fuel.
Each tremor, each insecurity, is a spark pointing to attachment — an opportunity for awakening.
If you chase fear away, it multiplies.
If you look at it with still awareness, it melts.

Awareness is the water that extinguishes the fire of fear.
It cools the burning illusion that "I am in danger," revealing instead:

"The body may perish, but the consciousness that perceives it cannot."

Once this is understood, even the thought of death becomes a form of meditation.

The Gift of Impermanence

Paradoxically, it is only because of death that life shines so vividly.
The petals of a flower are beautiful precisely because they fade.
Moments matter because they will not return.
Death is what gives life its sacred intensity — the reminder to awaken *now*.

The wise do not mourn impermanence; they bow to it.
They know that eternity expresses itself through change.
When you embrace impermanence, you do not lose life — you gain all of it.

Nachiketa's Crossing

Through Yama's teaching, Nachiketa attains fearlessness.
He no longer seeks to avoid death; he understands it.
In that understanding, he transcends it.
His consciousness becomes still, radiant, unmoved by coming or going.

In the stillness of realization, he discovers that the *knower of death* cannot die.
He has crossed the river — not by escaping it, but by dissolving the idea of separation.

Reflection Practice

Tonight, sit quietly in a darkened room.
Close your eyes and bring awareness to your breath.
Contemplate:

"If this were my last breath, what would remain?"

Do not think — feel.
See that awareness itself does not end when breath pauses.
That awareness *is* the eternal, watching the rhythm of life and death as one continuous wave.

Closing Insight

Fear is not conquered by courage — it is dissolved by clarity.
Death is not darkness — it is a doorway.
And the soul, once awakened, walks through it not trembling, but luminous.

For the wise, life and death are two mirrors reflecting the same light.
The Self is the flame that burns in both.

Awakening to the Real

Living with the Awareness of Immortality

To awaken is not to escape the world — it is to see it as it truly is.

When Nachiketa returned from the abode of Yama, he did not become otherworldly or detached.

He lived among people, walked the same earth, breathed the same air —

but everything he saw shimmered with meaning.

He was awake.

Yama's teaching had not given him new beliefs.

It had unveiled *Reality* — not something beyond the world, but something within it.

The veil had dropped, and what was once seen as ordinary now revealed the extraordinary presence of the eternal.

This is the transformation that happens when one truly knows the Self.

The Real and the Unreal

Yama had said:

"The eternal is not attained by the transient.

The Real is known only by turning away from the unreal."

What is unreal?
It is that which changes — the body, emotions, possessions, reputations, memories.
What is Real?
That which remains unchanged through all change — the awareness that perceives it all.

This is not a philosophical distinction; it is an experiential one.
When you observe your thoughts without identifying with them, you touch the Real.
When you feel emotion without drowning in it, you touch the Real.
When you love without possession, create without attachment, or act without anxiety — you live from the Real.

To awaken is to live *as* that awareness, even in the midst of change.

Seeing Through the World

After realization, the world does not disappear — illusion does.
You still see form, but now you see the formless shining through it.
You still hear sound, but you recognize silence within it.
You still act, but you know the actor and the action are one.

The awakened do not abandon the marketplace; they walk through it in peace.
They no longer seek eternity in time or fulfillment in things.
Instead, they see every moment as an expression of the Infinite —

a wave arising and dissolving in the same ocean.

Freedom Within Action

Yama taught that the wise do not escape karma; they act without bondage.
Freedom is not inaction — it is *awakened action.*

It is doing what must be done without ego, fear, or desire for result.

This is the state of **Karmayoga**, where every act becomes sacred.

Cooking, writing, teaching, healing, even resting — all are movements of the same divine energy, guided by awareness rather than compulsion.

To live like this is to transform life into worship.

Not of a god outside, but of the presence within all things.

The Radiance of the Ordinary

When consciousness awakens, the smallest acts become luminous.

A breath feels infinite.

A cup of water carries the reflection of eternity.

A stranger's face reveals the same Self you once sought in scriptures.

The awakened person no longer seeks miracles — for life itself is the miracle.

There is no higher or lower, no sacred or profane.

The real saint is not one who withdraws, but one who sees divinity in the dust.

The Death of Desire

When the Self is known, desire loses its fever.

Not because one represses it, but because fulfillment has already been found.

The ocean no longer thirsts for rivers.

This is not apathy; it is plenitude.

The heart overflows naturally into compassion, service, and creativity —

but now, nothing is needed in return.

Love becomes unconditional, work becomes joy, and even solitude feels complete.

Desire dies, and in its place, *devotion* is born.

Living in Two Worlds

To live awakened is to dwell in two dimensions simultaneously.
In one, you engage with form — speaking, thinking, loving, acting.
In the other, you rest as the formless — pure, silent awareness.

The two are not separate.
They coexist like the wave and the ocean.
You move through time while rooted in the timeless.

This balance is the highest yoga — to be fully human yet fully divine,
to live in the world without being trapped by it.

The Light That Never Dies

The Katha Upanishad describes the Self as:

"The light of lights, beyond darkness.
He who knows this, shining within the heart,
leaves sorrow far behind."

This is not poetic exaggeration; it is precise mystic observation.
The "light" is awareness itself — the luminosity by which all perception happens.
Even in deep sleep, even at the moment of death, this light does not fade.

When you realize that this light is your own essence, death becomes a shadow passing across your brilliance — not the end of it.

The Modern Sage

In today's world, the awakened person may not look different from anyone else.
They may run a business, raise children, write poetry, heal bodies, build systems.
But inwardly, everything they do arises from stillness.

Their actions are effortless because they flow from truth, not tension.

The true sign of awakening is *simplicity*.

There is no superiority, no claim of enlightenment — only the natural peace of being what one has always been.

The Presence of the Eternal

When awareness becomes your resting state, time loses its tyranny.

You no longer measure life in years, but in moments of pure presence.

You are not anxious to arrive anywhere — because the destination is always *here*.

The awakened do not live *for* something; they live *from* something — the inexhaustible well of the Self.

Every breath becomes prayer.

Every silence becomes communion.

Every act becomes creation.

This is immortality in daily life — eternity expressed as existence.

Reflection Practice

Sit quietly and watch your thoughts move like clouds.

Notice the space in which they appear — vast, open, untouched.

Ask yourself gently:

"What is aware of this thought?"

"Does that awareness age, fear, or end?"

Rest in that recognition.

You are not the cloud; you are the sky.

You are not the moment; you are the timeless witness in which moments rise and fall.

Closing Insight

Immortality is not the conquest of death — it is the remembrance of life's eternal essence.

To awaken is to see that everything you sought was already

within you,
and everything you feared was only a shadow upon your light.

This is the secret Nachiketa carried back to the world — that the highest wisdom does not distance us from life, it deepens our love for it.

For when the Self awakens, it no longer seeks to live forever — it simply knows it *always has.*

The Light That Never Dies

Integrating the Eternal into the Modern World

When the Upanishadic sages spoke of immortality, they were not speaking of endless time.

They were describing **timelessness** — a dimension of consciousness beyond change, decay, and becoming.

To realize this truth is one thing; to *live* it amidst the noise of modern life is another.

Yet that is the true test of wisdom: can the eternal be brought into the transient without losing its purity?

This is what we now explore — how the **light that never dies** can illuminate the world of constant change.

The Return of the Seer

Nachiketa's journey is complete — yet it is also just beginning.

He has crossed the threshold of death, touched the immortal flame, and returned to the world of men.

He does not withdraw into isolation or become a preacher of dogma.

He lives *as* the realization — silent, luminous, grounded.

In this, he becomes the archetype of the modern sage:
one who carries eternity lightly,

who walks through the world with a calm that transforms without effort.

Each of us is called to become a modern Nachiketa —
not ascetics on a mountain, but awakened souls in motion,
weaving timeless awareness through the fabric of time.

The Light in the Lab and the Market

The same Self that dwells in meditation also dwells in the laboratory, the classroom, the hospital, the boardroom.
When awareness becomes your foundation, work becomes worship.

Science, when guided by this inner clarity, no longer seeks to dominate nature but to understand her.
Business becomes not exploitation, but exchange — energy circulating for mutual upliftment.
Technology, when built from awareness, serves consciousness rather than consuming it.

To bring the eternal into the modern is not to abandon progress —
it is to **humanize it**.
It is to ensure that advancement serves awakening rather than addiction.

Relationships as Sacred Mirrors

When the Self is realized, relationships cease to be transactions and become reflections.
You no longer seek completion in another; you celebrate recognition.
The beloved, the friend, the stranger — all become mirrors of the same luminous consciousness.

Love loses its tension and gains its tenderness.
It is no longer born of lack, but of overflow.
The awakened one loves because they cannot *not* love —
the heart has become a sun.

Even conflict becomes sacred, for it reveals where illusion still lingers.
Thus, every relationship becomes a field of growth,
a dialogue of the divine with itself.

The Death of Division

Modern civilization thrives on separation — between science and spirit, human and nature, self and other.
But once the light of awareness dawns, division dissolves.
The scientist and the sage become one: both exploring reality, one through matter, the other through mind.
The artist and the mystic become one: both giving form to the formless.

The awakening of the Self is not a retreat from the world, but the healing of the world's fractures through the recognition of unity.

This is the true revolution — not political, but perceptual.
For when perception changes, systems follow.

The Art of Presence in a Fragmented Age

In a world addicted to speed, stillness is rebellion.
To be fully *present* in conversation, in work, in love —
that is to bring eternity into time.

Presence is the living flame of immortality.
It transforms every act into sacred participation.
When you are present, you are not merely living;
you are allowing the universe to live through you consciously.

This is what the Katha Upanishad foresaw —
not the escape of the few, but the awakening of the many,
a civilization built upon awareness rather than anxiety.

Leadership of the Awakened

The leader of tomorrow is not one who dominates, but one who radiates.
Their power does not come from control, but from coherence —
the harmony between word, action, and being.

Such a person leads without hierarchy because they are rooted in wholeness.
Their clarity itself becomes contagion.
In their presence, others awaken to their own light.

This is the leadership of Yama — fierce truth delivered with compassion.
It is the leadership of Nachiketa — fearless inquiry held in innocence.

Every awakened being becomes such a leader,
whether they guide a family, a classroom, or a nation.

Art, Creation, and the Immortal Vision

When the artist touches the Self, creation becomes revelation.
Art ceases to be self-expression and becomes *Self-expression* —
the Infinite pouring itself through color, sound, or word.

Music becomes meditation.
Writing becomes transmission.
Architecture becomes prayer in stone.

The Upanishadic consciousness does not destroy creativity;
it sanctifies it.
Every brushstroke, every invention, every insight becomes a hymn to the eternal.

The modern world needs such art —
not as decoration, but as remembrance.

The Healing of the Earth

Yama, as the Lord of Order, symbolizes balance —
and today, his wisdom whispers again through the voice of the planet.
Our ecological crisis is a spiritual crisis —
a forgetting of our shared being with all life.

When we remember the Self, we remember that the tree breathes for us,

that the river flows *through* us,
that the earth is not beneath our feet, but within our very body.

To heal the planet, we must awaken from the illusion of separateness.
Consciousness and ecology are one.
This is not philosophy; it is survival.

Modern Spirituality: From Belief to Being

In an age overflowing with spiritual information, what we lack is *transformation.*
Real spirituality is not accumulation but *subtraction* — the removal of illusion.

To integrate the eternal into modern life means to shift from concepts to consciousness,
from belief to direct experience.
When you live as awareness, religion becomes irrelevant,
for you have discovered the sacred in yourself and in everything.

This is not the death of religion; it is its fulfillment.

Reflection Practice

As you move through your day, pause often and silently ask:

"Who is experiencing this moment?"

Feel the answer — not in thought, but in awareness itself.
Let the question dissolve into presence.

Whether you are speaking, typing, driving, or resting,
sense the same silent flame within you and around you.
That flame has no name, no age, no beginning, and no end.

Closing Insight

The light that never dies is not elsewhere —
it is what looks through your eyes right now.
To live in remembrance of that light is to live consciously, compassionately, creatively.

This is the new spirituality —
ancient in essence, modern in expression,
rooted in awareness yet flowering in action.

When humanity learns to see with the eyes of Nachiketa,
Yama's kingdom will no longer be feared.
For then, even in the midst of endings,
we will know —
nothing real can ever die.

The Eternal Now

The Immortal Within You

The journey that began with a question — *What happens after death?* — ends not in an answer, but in awakening. Nachiketa's dialogue with Yama, the Lord of Death, reveals what every human heart secretly longs to know:
that immortality is not something to be reached beyond life, but something to be *realized within life.*

The search for eternity ends in the discovery of the **Eternal Now** —
a dimension of being where the river of time flows through the ocean of timelessness,
and every moment glows with the same undying presence.

Time and the Timeless

Yama tells Nachiketa:

"The Self is neither born nor does it die.
It did not come from anywhere, nor will it go anywhere.
It is unborn, eternal, everlasting, ancient —
and when the body is slain, it is not slain."

In this truth lies the foundation of freedom.
The Self does not move through time; time moves through the Self.
The same awareness that watched your childhood now watches this very moment — unchanged, unaged, unbound.

The mind divides past and future; awareness sees only *now*. When you rest in this awareness, you discover that eternity has always been here —
patiently waiting behind your distractions,
like sunlight behind clouds.

The End of Seeking

Every journey of the soul begins with seeking — for meaning, for love, for peace.
But when realization dawns, the seeker disappears,
and what remains is seeing.

The wave that searched for the ocean realizes —
it was never apart.

This is the stillness the sages called *moksha* — liberation not in the afterlife, but in this life.
It is not withdrawal; it is intimacy with all that is.
It is to breathe without fear, to love without reason,
to live without resistance.

The Everyday Immortal

The awakened person does not glow with halo or miracle. They walk through the marketplace, answer the phone, cook meals, write letters, dream, laugh, weep —
yet through it all, they remain unshaken by circumstance.

For them, birth and death are scenes in the same play.
Gain and loss, joy and sorrow — all waves in the same sea.
They live in the center of impermanence as one lives in the eye of a storm — still, silent, untouched.

Such a person is not superhuman — only fully human,
for they have remembered what humanity truly is:
the meeting point of the finite and the infinite.

The Sacred Breath

The sages often called breath the bridge between body and soul.

Every inhalation is life entering form;
every exhalation is form returning to formlessness.

To live consciously is to honor this rhythm —
to feel the pulse of eternity moving through each breath.

When you breathe with awareness, you are communing with the very mystery Yama revealed.
You are not practicing spirituality;
you are embodying it.

Awareness in Action

The Eternal Now is not a passive state; it is dynamic stillness. When you act from awareness, every movement carries intelligence, every word carries healing.
You no longer act to prove or acquire,
but to express the fullness already within you.

Work becomes worship.
Silence becomes eloquence.
Time becomes the theater through which timelessness dances.

This is the secret of immortality in motion —
to move while resting in the unmoving center.

Death as Continuum

The wise see death not as an event but as a transition —
a doorway from one state of awareness to another.
Just as sleep is not the end of waking,
death is not the end of life.
It is simply the Self changing its instrument of experience.

In this realization, grief softens.
You still love, you still remember, you still feel —
but beneath it all, you know: *no one ever truly goes anywhere.*
Consciousness only changes form.
The melody continues in a different octave.

Immortality as Intimacy

The immortality spoken of in the Katha Upanishad is not distance from the world; it is deeper intimacy with it.

When you see the same Self in all beings,
you no longer feel separate from anything.

The flower blooming, the rain falling, the child laughing, the old man resting —
all become reflections of the same infinite awareness.
You see that life is not happening *to* you —
it is happening *as* you.

To know this is to live in ceaseless wonder.

The Still Heart

At the end of the dialogue, Yama blesses Nachiketa, saying:

"This knowledge is the secret of secrets,
the supreme path of peace.
Whoever realizes this Self becomes immortal here and now."

Notice — *here and now.*
Immortality is not a future promise; it is a present realization.
It is available in this breath, this heartbeat, this awareness reading these words.

The heart that rests in this knowing is beyond turbulence.
It does not cling, for it sees that all belongs.
It does not fear, for it knows that nothing is ever lost.

The Eternal Now in Modern Life

To live the Eternal Now in our era is to awaken within complexity —
to remember stillness amid speed,
presence amid information,
truth amid opinion.

Every moment becomes a doorway back to the Self.
When you stop waiting for a "spiritual moment," you realize every moment is spiritual.

As you walk, drive, speak, or listen — awareness remains the same.
This continuity is immortality.

Reflection Practice

Pause now.

Let go of every effort to understand.

Simply be aware — of your breath, your body, the sounds around you.

Ask inwardly:

"Am I aware of being aware?"

Rest in that awareness.

Feel its stillness, its depth, its clarity.

That awareness is untouched by birth or death.

That is *you.*

Stay here — in the Eternal Now —

and know that eternity has never been elsewhere.

Closing Insight

Immortality is not the extension of life — it is the expansion of awareness.

The secret Yama gave to Nachiketa is the secret life gives to all who listen:

that the deathless dwells within the dying,

the infinite hides within the finite,

and heaven is not a destination but a perception.

The Upanishad ends not with a farewell, but with a beginning —

for one who knows the Self never ends.

The journey is complete,

and yet — it is forever unfolding.

You are that flame.

You are that silence.

You are that which never began

and will never cease to be.

Welcome home to the Eternal Now.

Epilogue

Living as the Eternal

The final teaching of the *Katha Upanishad* is not in its words, but in its silence.
After all the questions and answers, after death has revealed its secret,
what remains is stillness — luminous, infinite, intimate.

It is the same stillness that exists between two breaths,
between two thoughts,
between two heartbeats.

That stillness is the *you* that does not come or go.

The Return Home

Every spiritual journey is a circle.
We leave home seeking truth, only to return and discover that truth was our very nature.
The road was only a mirror leading us back to ourselves.

Nachiketa returned from his meeting with Yama not as a prophet, but as a presence —
ordinary in appearance, extraordinary in awareness.
He had crossed the river of fear and realized there was never another shore.

You, too, have walked that circle in these pages.
And perhaps now you glimpse what he saw:

that the eternal was never hidden — only unseen through the fog of forgetfulness.

The Realization to Live By

When you wake each morning, remind yourself:

"I am the awareness that witnesses change."

See how fear begins to fade,
how gratitude begins to rise.
For when you remember the eternal, the temporary becomes sacred — not because it lasts,
but because it glows with the light of what does.

Let every act — your work, your love, your stillness — become a prayer of remembrance.
Live with open eyes, knowing that every person you meet is another form of the same consciousness.

That is immortality in practice — not the rejection of life,
but its sanctification.

The Light Continues

The *Katha Upanishad* ends, but its flame does not.
It burns quietly in every question, in every act of courage, in every moment of awareness.
It reminds us that enlightenment is not the privilege of the few
—
it is the birthright of all who dare to look within.

When you live as the eternal,
you no longer seek to be remembered —
for you have become remembrance itself.

Final Blessing

May this book not give you answers,
but awaken the silence in which answers arise.

May you walk the path of Nachiketa — fearless, sincere, luminous.

And when life brings its endings — as it always does — may you smile, knowing that endings are only beginnings returning home.

For you are not the traveler,
nor the road,
nor the destination.

You are the **light that never dies.**

About the Author

Dr. Surabhi Solanki is a physician, writer, and spiritual explorer whose life bridges the worlds of science, healing, and ancient wisdom.

Throughout her career in medicine, she has witnessed the fragility and brilliance of human life — moments where the boundary between life and death becomes astonishingly thin. These experiences awakened in her a deep curiosity: *What truly lives within us? What remains untouched by birth, illness, or time?*

Her search for answers led her beyond the stethoscope and into the heart of India's spiritual tradition. Drawn to the clarity and courage of the Upanishads, she immersed herself in their teachings, discovering that the wisdom they carry is not old — it is eternal, alive, and urgently needed in the modern world.

As a writer, Dr. Solanki brings a rare blend of compassion, clarity, and poetic insight. She has the gift of translating profound spiritual truths into language that feels intimate, accessible, and transformative. Her voice is rooted in authenticity — simple yet powerful, modern yet timeless.

Through her work, she guides readers toward self-inquiry, stillness, and inner freedom. She invites each person to look beyond the noise of the mind and discover the luminous presence that has always been there: the immortal Self.

Dr. Solanki believes that every human being carries a spark of the infinite — and that spiritual awakening is not the privilege of the few, but the birthright of all.

With each book, each teaching, each reflection, she offers a gentle reminder:

You are far more than a body living through time.
You are the light that time cannot touch.

Official Website: drsurabhisolanki.com
Email: drsurabhisolanki@gmail.com

9 789355 921826

Printed at Repro India Ltd.

CAPYBARA For Kids

Fun Facts, photos & Fascinating info about the world's largest rodent.

Published by
GRAPEVINE BOOKS

www.grapevinebooks.com
email: contact@grapevinebooks.com
Ordering Information:
Quantity sales: Special discounts are available on quantity purchases
by corporations, associations, and others.
For details, reach out to the publisher.

First published by Grapevine Books 2025